SOLID

KIM THOMPSON

A Crabtree Roots Book

Crabtree Publishing

crabtreebooks.com

School-to-Home Support for Caregivers and Teachers

This book helps children grow by letting them practice reading. Here are a few guiding questions to help the reader with building his or her comprehension skills. Possible answers appear here in red.

Before Reading:

• What do I think this book is about?
  • *I think this book is about things you can touch.*
  • *I think this book is about things things we use every day.*

• What do I want to learn about this topic?
  • *I want to learn what* solid *means.*
  • *I want to learn how to tell the difference between a solid and something else.*

During Reading:

• I wonder why...
  • *I wonder how many things around me are solids.*
  • *I wonder what other kinds of matter there can be.*

• What have I learned so far?
  • *I have learned that solid things have a shape.*
  • *I have learned that you can weigh things that are solids.*

After Reading:

• What details did I learn about this topic?
  • *I have learned that solid things can feel hard or soft.*
  • *I have learned that ice is solid water.*

• Read the book again and look for the vocabulary words.
  • *I see the word* **matter** *on page 3 and the word* **solid** *on page 4. The other vocabulary words are found on page 14.*

All things are **matter**.

Some matter is **solid**.

shelf

shirt

spoon

carrot

bowl

A solid has **weight**.

A solid keeps its **shape** if you move it.

Solids can **feel** hard or soft.

Ice is solid water.

Is water always a solid?

How could you change it?

Word List
Sight Words

a	has	move
all	if	soft
and	is	some
are	it	things
can	its	water
hard	keeps	you

Words to Know

feel   **ice**   **matter**

shape   **solid**   **weight**

All things are **matter**.

Some matter is **solid**.

A solid has **weight**.

A solid keeps its **shape** if you move it.

Solids can **feel** hard or soft.

Ice is solid water.

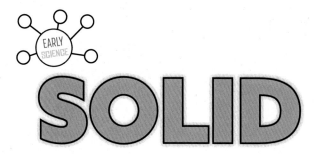

Written by: Kim Thompson

Designed by: Rhea Wallace

Series Development: James Earley

Proofreader: Kathy Middleton

Educational Consultant: Marie Lemke M.Ed.

Photographs:
Shutterstock: Africa Studio: cover; Sumate Gulabutdee:
   p. 1; Pro-stock Studio: p. 3, 5; Eastimages: p. 7;
   brizmaker: p. 9; Somdul: p. 10; Yellowcat: p. 13

Crabtree Publishing

crabtreebooks.com   800-387-7650

Printed in Canada/112023/20231130

Published in Canada
Crabtree Publishing
616 Welland Ave.
St. Catharines, Ontario
L2M 5V6

Published in the United States
Crabtree Publishing
347 Fifth Ave
Suite 1402-145
New York, NY 10016

Library and Archives Canada Cataloguing in Publication
Available at Library and Archives Canada

Library of Congress Cataloging-in-Publication Data
Available at the Library of Congress

Hardcover: 978-1-0398-0969-7
Paperback: 978-1-0398-1022-8
Ebook (pdf): 978-1-0398-1128-7
Epub: 978-1-0398-1075-4